CULTIVATE YOUR

cashflow

Create a Money-Making Marketing Plan Using Human Design

A companion workbook to the book, *Cultivate You!*

Lise Cartwright | HustleandGroove.com

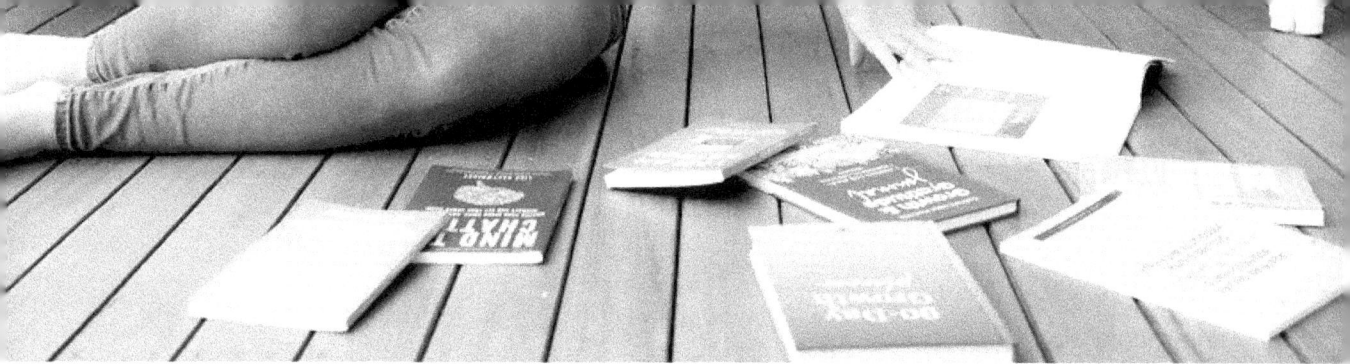

Hello Creative Business Owner

Are you ready to create a consistent income business based on what FEELS easy and fun for you?

With this workbook you will be able to create an action plan to that brings you consistent income month after month. No more feast or famine cycles for you!

You've made a great decision, here's why...

✓ Creating an online business that harnesses your strengths allows you to focus on the tactics and strategies that feel easy and fun for you. It allows you to connect with your audience in a way that comes **natural** to you. This leads to easy cash flow and no one-size-fits-all strategies in sight!

✓ When you combine your you-nique gifts, strengths, and talents to craft your messages, you're able to step into truly authentic content and offers that resonates with your people. You don't need to use fancy words or fancy tactics to attract your ideal customer. Be you. Show that you genuinely care. Empower and inspire your audience by sharing the authentic, raw you. Since you're here to truly make a difference in the lives of your people, they are much more likely to want to buy more from—and work with—someone they feel they **connect** with.

✓ On top of being easy and fun, when you focus on you doing you in your business, you're able to **sell** to your audience will ease. By leaning into being more you, you stand out in your space because you're creating offers that provide value and changes lives. Marketing your business doesn't mean you need to sell your soul. Instead, when you do what comes naturally to you, cash flows freely.

Contents
it's time to discover what's inside!

Congratulations on purchasing this **Workbook!** If you haven't purchased the first book in this series, *Cultivate You!*, please do that here to get the best experience: www.hustleandgroove.com/cybbook

Do what feels right to you, not what someone else tells you works. Listen to what lights you up and create from that space...

LISE CARTWRIGHT, BEST SELLING AUTHOR AND CREATIVE BUSINESS COACH

Introduction
you do you!

Since starting my business in 2011, I have strived for consistent cash flow.

I don't know what your experience has been like with this, but mine resembled the feast or famine cycle.

I could go months barely making ends meet (famine) and then the next few months would be crazy (feast) and I'd be on a high from all the money that was flowing in.

But I could never get it consistent.

That is, until 2022 rolled around.

Aside from the craziness that hit the world, I made the biggest discovery that changed the trajectory of my life and business.

Human Design.

Whether you believe in it or not, doesn't really matter.

What Human Design showed me was how I could run my business my way.

How I could do things that were *easy and fun* for me.

Once I started applying this to my business, it completely changed everything...

When I understood what easy and fun looked like for me, consistent cash flow became the norm.

Introduction
you do you!

Once I had consistent cash flow, I could make decisions based on what felt good vs. what would bring me the most amount of money.

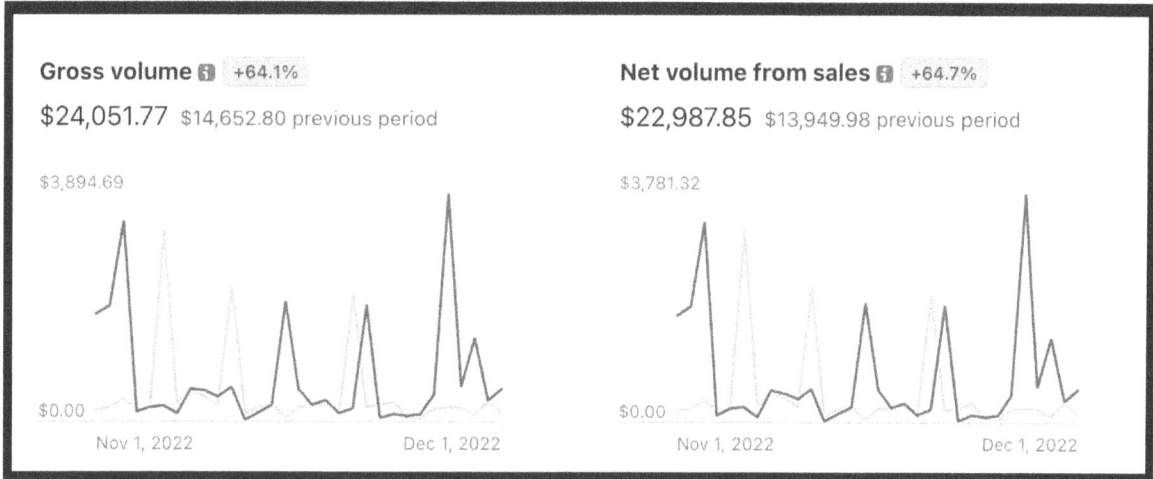

Gross volume +64.1%

$24,051.77 $14,652.80 previous period

$3,894.69

$0.00

Nov 1, 2022   Dec 1, 2022

Net volume from sales +64.7%

$22,987.85 $13,949.98 previous period

$3,781.32

$0.00

Nov 1, 2022   Dec 1, 2022

It was freeing.

It's what led me to create a course called *Human Design For Business* and course called the *Cultivate Group Coaching Program*.

And since then, I've also helped other creative entrepreneurs craft businesses that are easy and fun for them.

Focused on their you-nique gifts, strengths, and talents.

No more following one-size-fits-all strategies and tactics.

If you've ever felt like there was something wrong...

Introduction
you do you!

Like you'd missed some special memo that listed all the secrets to money making or lacked the skills to make money online, this workbook is for you.

When read in combination with my other book, *Cultivate You! Harness Your Strengths, Craft Your Message, and Market With Ease*, you have the exact knowledge and framework that I used to create consistent income in my business.

It's also what my members have used over and over again to create their own businesses that are easy, fun, AND profitable.

So grab your colored pens, pencils, and highlighters and let's dive in.

It's time to create consistent income months for your business.

Let's do it!

Cultivate Your Cashflow
daily money-making activities

These are the activities that will allow you to grow and scale your business with ease.

There are three core areas that make up your daily money-making activities:

1. **Growing** your audience & offers
2. **Nurturing** your audience
3. **Selling** to your audience

Over the next few pages, we'll explore each of these areas and how you can incorporate these into your 90-day money-making marketing plan.

CHAPTER ONE

growing activities

ideas...

ideas...

Growing your audience and offers is the most important aspect of your daily money-making activities.

*For initial guidance on how you'll create offers, check your human design chart and the gates you have active in the **Sacral Center**.*

*If you're looking for a direction to take your offers in, review your chart again and look to your **G Center**. What gates are active there?*

Dive into the main book, Cultivate You!, and visit chapter seven "The Three Business Centers" for more details

Without an audience, you have no-one to sell to.

Without offers, you have nothing to sell.

It's a little like the 'chicken or egg debate—which comes first?

While I can't help with the chicken or egg debate, I can help you decide what to focus your GROW efforts on...

The easiest place to start is based on your phase of business.

Inside the Cultivate Group Coaching Program, I have roadmaps created based on each phase of business with a 'persona' attached to each.

Here's what they are:

- **Startup Sally** - You're in this phase if you've just started your business and have no email list, no offers, no website OR you're making less than $1,000 per month.

- **Launching Lucy** - You're in this phase if you've got 1-2 low-cost offers, a small email list (1,000 subscribers or less), your website is live, and you're looking to launch a mid-to-high ticket offer or recurring income model.

- **Growing Gabby** - You're in this phase if you've got multiple offers at varying prices, an email list with 3,000+ email subscribers OR you're making more than $2k per month.

- **Money-Making Mary** - You're in this phase if you've got multiple offers at varying prices, an email list with 5,000+ subscribers OR you're making $5k or more per month.

Based on each of those phases, you'll likely be more focused on growing your audience or growing your offer suite.

Personally, I'm in the *Money-Making Mary phase* of my business and yet, I still focus on growing my audience every day. This is because, for my business, people are everything.

Based on each phase, here's what your daily GROW activities might include:

STARTUP SALLY
Your first decision will be on HOW you want to grow your audience. There are many ways, but the two that I recommend to my members are:

1. Run **lead generation ads** on Facebook and Instagram. You can get started with those for as little as $5 a day and depending on your targeting and budget, you'll have anywhere from 20-50 people per week joining your email list.
2. **Joint list-building events**. These events typically run anywhere from 48 hours to 5 days. On average, you can add 100+ subscribers to your email list from just one event. These events are free.

Because we're talking about DAILY activities, you might also share your lead magnet (the incentive to get people onto your email list) on your social media platforms each day.

Or you could run lead generation ads and tweak them each week.

At the same time, you'd be looking to grow your offer suite. The fastest way to do this is to 'get paid to create'.

This is the easiest way to ensure that the offers you've mapped out will actually sell.

Getting paid to create is where you pre-sell your offer and validate it with the first 5+ sales. Only then do you create it.

Here's the high-level overview of what that looks like:

1. You complete the Tangible Offer Framework (located inside the *Cultivate Your Offers* workbook) for the offer you're planning to create.
2. You pull together a short sales page or checkout page with a video that explains what the offer is and when they will get it.
3. You share a simple post on social media or send an email that simply states "I'm thinking about hosting a live workshop on how to create a money-making marketing plan. It's $27. You in?" It doesn't have to be a workshop; you'd put whatever container you're using to deliver in place of a "live workshop".
4. Anyone that responds to your social media post or email with a "yes, I'm in" you share the payment link with.
5. Once you have at least 5 sales of the offer, only then do you CREATE it.

If you get less than five sales, it's up to you whether you move forward with the offer or not.

If you get NO sales, then you haven't wasted your time creating something nobody wants!

When building out your 90-day plan, you'll likely spend the first 90-days focused on the GROW phase.

Grow your audience. Grow your offers.

Then get ready to dive into the next phase.

LAUNCHING LUCY
You're in this phase because you're getting ready to launch a new offer out to the world.

Your focus will be to GROW your audience.

Your daily activities are simple. Bring people into your world every day.

The fastest way to do this would be to run lead generation ads. You'd want to budget $10-$15 per day to grow your audience by 100+ subscribers each week.

The goal of these ads would be to have a strategic freebie that opens the gap for your upcoming offer.

For example, if you're launching a membership within the next 90 days, your strategic freebie could be a tangible deliverable that you have inside the membership.

As they access the strategic freebie, you'd invite them to join the waitlist for your membership (particularly if you're a Projector!).

You could test multiple strategic freebies in the first 30 days to see which one brings in the most amount of people for the lowest cost.

You'll also want to ensure that you are dialing in on the NURTURE phase (which we'll cover in the next chapter), too.

GROWING GABBY
Your decision about what to focus on in this phase will largely be based on what's working for you right now and what's not.

If you have 3,000+ email subscribers but only a 20% open rate, then you might want to bring new people into your world and remove cold subscribers.

If you have several offers but they aren't selling, then you might look to follow the 'get paid to create' process to see what your audience resonates with.

If you choose to GROW your email list, lead generation ads at $5-$10 a day would be a good option as well as participating in/hosting 1-2 joint promotion list-building events.

If you choose to GROW your offer suite, follow the pre-selling process below:

1. Complete the Tangible Offer Framework (located inside the *Cultivate Your Offers workbook*) for the offer you're planning to create.
2. Create a short sales page or checkout page with a video that explains what the offer is and when they will get it.
3. Share a simple post on social media or send an email that simply states "I'm thinking about hosting a live workshop on how to create a money-making marketing plan. It's $27. You in?" It doesn't have to be a workshop, you'd put whatever container you're using to deliver in place of a "live workshop".
4. Anyone that responds to your social media post or email with a "yes, I'm in", receives the link to your payment page.
5. Once you've made at least 5 sales of the offer, only then do you CREATE it.

If you make less than five sales, it's up to you whether you move forward with the offer or not.

If you get NO sales, then you haven't wasted your time creating something nobody wants! Go back to the drawing board and repeat this process until you find something that sticks.

MONEY-MAKING MARY
The decision you're making here is largely going to depend on your business model.

*If you have a **recurring income model** (like a membership, subscription, mastermind etc) then you'll likely be focusing on bringing new people into your world every day, while refining your content to reduce your churn rate*

*If you're a **coach**, you might be focused on building out your offer suite with smaller, low-cost offers to meet the needs of your audience before they are ready to work with you one-on-one*

*If you're a **non-fiction author**, you might be focused on creating a group coaching program that takes your book(s) concepts deeper and with more actionable, tangible results.*

My recommendation?

At a minimum, GROW your audience every day through lead generation ads. $5-$10 a day is a great budget to keep new people coming into your world while you continue to serve your customers/clients/members.

No matter what GROW focus you're doing, knowing your numbers is key to help you decide.

The *Income Projection Calculator* (located in the resource hub) will give you a clear picture on whether you need to grow your audience or your offer suite.

No matter what you're doing, add these activities to your 90-Day Plan.

Now that you've got your daily GROW activities mapped out, let's dive into one of the most overlooked areas in our businesses.

Nurturing our audiences!

GROW Daily Activities
exercise time

To determine your GROW activities, it starts with understanding which phase of business you're in right now. Read the explanations below and jot down which one you're in.

Startup Sally - *You're in this phase if you've just started your business and have no email list, no offers, no website OR you're making less than $1,000 per month.*

Launching Lucy - *You're in this phase if you've got 1-2 low-cost offers, a small email list (1,000 subscribers or less), your website is live, and you're looking to launch a mid-to-high ticket offer or recurring income model.*

Growing Gabby - *You're in this phase if you've got multiple offers at varying prices, an email list with 3,000+ email subscribers OR you're making more than $2k per month.*

Money-Making Mary - *You're in this phase if you've got multiple offers at varying prices, an email list with 5,000+ subscribers AND you're making $5k or more per month.*

GROW Daily Activities

exercise time

Based on your phase of business, jot down the activities that you'll do to GROW in either your offers or audience.

CHAPTER TWO

nurturing activities

ideas...

ideas...

Once you've grown your audience and offer suite, we need to keep our audience engaged.

*For initial guidance on developing your unique, authentic voice, look to the **Throat Center** and the gates you have active there. This will give you insights into the way you communicate to your audience.*

Dive into the main book, Cultivate You!, and visit chapter seven "The Three Business Centers" for more details

This is where I see my members struggling again and again.

Our Voxer Coaching Days are often filled with questions like:

- *"What do I say to my email subscribers?"*
- *"How do I come up with content for my newsletters?"*
- *"Do I have to be on social media?"*

There are two ways that I teach my members to come up with content for their emails (and socials if you're jiving with being there):

1. Create a Story bank.
2. Create Discoverable Content

Depending on your audience, you'll either be emailing them once a week, twice a month, or monthly.

But they need to hear from you (at least email wise) at a minimum of once a month.

Personally, I'd recommend a little more than that. But this is where you'll want to follow your strategy and authority in making that decision.

When I first started, I emailed my subscribers once a month.

Then I switched to once a week.

Then 2-3 times a week.

Now, I email them 5+ times a week.

I know you're probably thinking... *"Five times a week! That seems like a lot. What is she even saying?"*

Well, if you've been in my world, you will have already experienced what that looks like.

But this isn't about what I'm doing. **This is about you and your business.**

Let's address the first question: *what do I talk to my email subscribers about?*

Here, we can switch back to looking at things through the lens of our Human Design type and strategy.

MANIFESTORS: Your strategy is to INFORM. Unapologetically sharing what you feel the urge to create and move forward with. In business, this looks like sharing what you're excited about, what you're working on, what you can't wait to bring to life.

So, in your emails — share. Because whatever it is that you're up to, the people who gel with what you're saying will jump on board no matter what it is.

GENERATORS: Your strategy is to RESPOND. To respond to external ideas, to the things that the Universe puts in front of you. If it's a yes, then your excitement will overflow and magnetically attract those to you who gel with that energy.

In business, this looks like following your joy, regardless of whether it makes sense. Regardless of whether it applies to business. Through the art of sharing your joy, your people will connect with you and respond to your emails.

MANIFESTING GENERATORS: Your strategy is to RESPOND and INFORM. In business, this looks like you share what you're excited about while also giving your subscribers a heads-up on anything that might impact them.

For example, if you were planning to do a flash sale next week, you'd INFORM your email subscribers that this was coming their way. If you were looking to launch a new offer, you might like to create a waitlist and invite your subscribers to join it.

RESPOND to what the Universe puts in front of you and then INFORM your audience about what you're planning.

PROJECTORS: Your strategy is to be INVITED. This means that before you give advice, you've got to wait for the person to ask for it. In business, this means that you've also got to be recognized BEFORE you're invited.

Imagine yourself as a taxi... if your light isn't on, how can anyone hail you for a ride?

So, turn your light on; aka start sharing your insights, knowledge, and wisdom with your audience so that they can SEE you're the person that can help them... and then they'll INVITE you through clicking on your sales pages and more.

REFLECTORS: Your strategy is to FOLLOW THE LUNAR CYCLE. Because you're so open, you're being carried along by the Universe rather than being directed like the other types.

In business, this is about paying attention to each lunar cycle and seeing what feels right as you experience each phase of 'You' during that 29-day cycle.

When it comes to what to share with your email subscribers, follow your flow. What feels right to talk about right now?

As you start to craft your regular emails, see what resonates the most.

The next question we'll address is: *How do I come up with content for my newsletters?*

While you could simply follow your strategy as outlined above, I also wanted to share what I have my members do when they are struggling with this.

Create a Story Bank.

Your story bank is simply a collection of stories based on different phases you've gone through in business right through to the things that happen to you each day.

I encourage you to capture stories as often as you can.

I personally started out with a Google Doc to capture my 'starting stories' and for capturing my daily stories, I use the Otter.ai app.

To kick off your own story bank, answer the following questions *(you'll find the template and training inside the resources hub)*:

1. What's your business 'origin' story? Why did you start it? What triggered it? What happened on the journey to launching it?
2. What's a defining moment in your business so far?
3. What other significant stories have happened that have made an impact on your business?
4. Write your story from the perspective of Island A
5. Write your story from the perspective of Island B
6. Write your story that includes the tangible transformation

Once you've got these stories, you can use them to communicate with your audience.

Use them to create posts for social media, write blog posts, craft podcast episodes or YouTube videos.

I'd also recommend reviewing the Tangible Offer Framework (which you'll find inside the *Cultivate Your Offers workbook)* for each offer that you have, paying close attention to your Island A and Island B bullet points.

Why?

Because these can also be turned into content, particularly long-form content such as blog posts, podcast episodes or YouTube videos.

Once you have all this content, you can REPURPOSE it into your regular newsletters.

Here's an example:

I have over 400 blog posts written and about 50 YouTube videos. I don't 'do' social media.

I also have a large daily story bank on my Otter.ai app (as shown below).

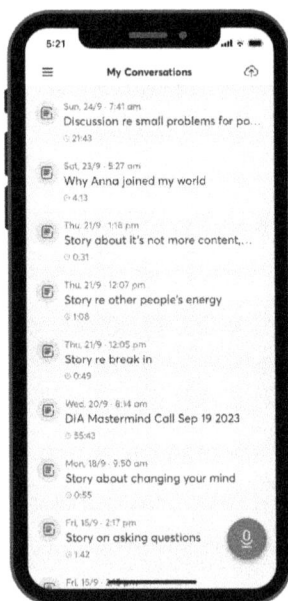

As I email almost daily, I don't struggle to come up with ideas because I have so much content to pull from.

In terms of what I decide to write in my emails?

I'm referring to my 90-day Money-Making Marketing Plan!

- *What am I promoting or launching?*
- *What do I want to share with my audience (following my gut)?*
- *How can I help them move closer to their goals?*

These are the questions I ask myself each day when I write my emails.

At the time of writing this book, Matthew Perry (star of the hit TV sitcom, Friends (Chandler Bing)) had passed away suddenly.

As someone who grew up watching Friends (it started airing when I was 16), I resonated so much with the storylines and its characters.

Over the following decade, I would switch between feeling like I was Rachael, then Monica, then Phoebe... always wishing I had male friends like Ross, Chandler, and Joey.

I felt compelled to share this story with my own audience.

Here's the email I wrote:

Subject: The one where I'm sad

Hey [FIRST NAME],

Honestly, I'm feeling a little sad.
I grew up with the cast of Friends and have been reading Matthew Perry's book for the last month or so.
I truly can't believe that he's gone.
Last night, I started rewatching Friends for the 100th time.
It made me feel better. More connected.
I thought it was weird that I felt such a profound sense of loss.
To feel this way about someone you've never met.
But it doesn't change the fact that Matthew Perry and the entire cast of Friends made an impact on my life.
I still watch the entire series at least once a year.
Hold your loved ones tight.
Tell people how much you care and appreciate them.
RIP Matthew Perry.

Take care.
Lise xoxo

As you can see, there was nothing to click, nothing to sell. Just sharing something with my audience. I received several email responses back.

Nurturing is about having human to human conversations... My audience isn't just a way for me to make money. I truly care about them and their success.

But what if you do want to sell?

Here's another example of what that might look like in a newsletter:

(You can see this in real life example here: https://ckarchive.com/b/xmuph6hrx0k6gbrnppvnqc0w0ezll).

This email doesn't actually sell anything... However, the video I've linked to is part of my Discoverable Content System (a program that's part of my membership).

When someone watches that video, it's optimized to invite them to check out the Cultivate Group Coaching Program membership.

Which leads me to the other part of the NURTURE process... having Discoverable Content.

What is Discoverable Content?

Discoverable Content is long-form content. This could be a blog post, a podcast episode, or a YouTube video.

Why I refer to this content as "discoverable" is based on the way you optimize this content.

Without getting too technical (because you just don't need to know it all for this to work), we want your long-form content to be easily discoverable by your ideal customers and potential customers.

But when they are searching for this content.

So, this is not about placing ads to get in front of your audience. This is organic.

Creating discoverable content starts with your offer suite.

The key is that we aren't creating content for the sake of creating content...

When I first started my business back in 2011, everyone was saying "content is king". In other words, if you created a ton of content, you'd be making money quickly.

I spent the better part of a year writing 4+ blog posts per month. It's why I have over 400 posts published on my website!

Here's the thing, though... you don't NEED 400+ blog posts.

I wish I could go back in time and tell 30-something Lise about the Discoverable Content System...

While I can't do that, I can help you.

Here's the high-level process to follow to create your own discoverable content:

- Review your offer suite. Which offers are always available and which offers are only available at certain times? Make a note.
- Do you have a Tangible Offer Framework document for each offer? If you don't, now's the time to create those. This is a key part of the system, so don't skip it...
- Looking at Island A, Island B bullet points, and the question around misconceptions and beliefs from your T.O.F. document—create a new document with that content in it.
- In this new document, what I like to call a 'messaging organizer', sit down and write down your thoughts as to why your audience has each pain point.

- In the same document, sit down and write down your thoughts as to how you can help your audience achieve Island B (obviously through the lens of your offer).
- In the same document, looking at misconceptions and beliefs, write down your thoughts as to why they think this and how your offer helps address these.
- Congratulations! You've just come up with all the starting points for your own Discoverable Content.

From here, you decide what long-form content you'll create to address as many of the items you've outlined in your document.

Here's a snapshot of what it might look like (taken from my *Cultivate Group Coaching Program* messaging organizer document).

Island A example:

- Struggling to figure out what offers to create and how to sell them BECAUSE the two pressure centres are playing havoc with their mind. Caught up with the ego, uncertainty is not what the ego likes, so feels overwhelmed, uncertain, stuck.
  - Content around the head and mind centres
  - Content around the three core centres and what it looks like when out of alignment

- Not sure what offers to create first. Do I need a certain number of offers? BECAUSE they aren't clear on what they want their business to look like. Not clear on their offer suite so can't move forward.
  - Content around how to choose offers that are in alignment with their ideal business
  - Content around the different types of business models and how to choose using your human design type

- How to build my email list without having to post in all the Facebook Groups BECAUSE they are following what someone else believes is the best way to build an email list instead of trusting their own way of doing business.
  - Content around how to make decisions that are in alignment with the way they want to run their business
  - Content around how to filter what you see other people doing through your unique approach - how you can tweak and modify anything once you know what's easy and fun for you

Island B example:

- HOW TO GO ABOUT: I know exactly what offers to create because I follow what feels good and selling happens almost on autopilot
  - I would explain how to use strategy and authority to make decisions in business
  - How to use your centres to help make decisions around what offers to create
- HOW TO GO ABOUT: I know what my offer suite is because I followed my strategy and authority and I listened to my audience.
  - How to survey your audience
  - How to find out what your audience is saying when you don't have an email list
  - What tools can help you listen to your audience
- HOW TO GO ABOUT: List building happens on autopilot since I discovered Lead Gen Ads and List Building Collaborations
  - Explain why lead gen ads are the best
  - Walk through list building collaborations
  - How to optimise your website for list building efforts

Once you've reached this point, you'd want to optimize your content based on the keyword phrases and search terms that attract your ideal customer.

This is where a little search engine optimization comes in.

A great resource to help you figure out keywords your audience is searching for is AnswerThePublic.com or a simple Google search.

Once you've got that information, you want to include that keyword phrase in your long-form content.

In the title, URL, meta description, and throughout the content.

Once that's done, then you schedule the sharing of that content to your social media profiles.

This content can also be repurposed in your regular emails with your audience.

It's about whatever feels easy and fun for you.

The whole point of your NURTURE activities is to let people know that you're a real human being, that you understand and 'get' your audience, and that you have offers to sell.

The best way to approach your newsletter content is to imagine you're having a conversation with a friend.

A new friend. Someone that doesn't know all your secrets...

And you're not sharing all your secrets (you definitely need some boundaries around what you do and don't share with your audience), but you are sharing things that impact you and your business.

Follow what feels easy and fun for you.

Remember this one rule: Your email list needs to hear from you at least once a month for them to remain 'warm' and for you to be top-of-mind.

RESOURCE: Story Bank Template & Training Video *(available inside the Resource Hub here: https://www.hustleandgroove.com/cycresources)*.

In the next chapter, we're going to talk about what it looks like to sell to your audience daily.

I know this is the chapter that you're excited to get to, so let's dive in!

NURTURE Daily Activities

exercise time

Once you've grown your audience and offer suite, we need to keep our audience engaged. We do that mainly through emails. Answer the questions below to start your own Story Bank.

- What's your business 'origin' story? Why did you start it? What triggered it? What happened on the journey to launching it?

- What's a defining moment in your business so far? Or what are multiple defining moments?

- What other significant stories have happened that have made an impact on you or your business?

- Write your story from the perspective of Island A (review the Tangible Offer Framework inside the workbook, *Cultivate Your Offers* if you're not sure what this is)

- Write your story from the perspective of Island B (review the Tangible Offer Framework inside the workbook, *Cultivate Your Offers* if you're not sure what this is)

- Write your story that includes the tangible transformation (review the Tangible Offer Framework if you're not sure what this is)

NURTURE Daily Activities

exercise time

Use the space below to kickstart your Story Bank stories...

CHAPTER THREE

selling activities

ideas...

ideas...

Once you've got your **GROW** and **NURTURE** daily activities mapped out, the next part of the process is to sell to your audience.

*For initial guidance on how you best sell, aside from following strategy and authority, review your chart and pay attention to the **Throat Center** gates. These will give you an idea on how you can sell with ease.*

*If you're looking for a direction to take your marketing in, review your chart again and look to your **G Center**. What gates are active there?*

Dive into the main book, Cultivate You!, and visit chapter seven "The Three Business Centers" for more details

Before we dive into what that looks like, let's do a bit of a mindset reset.

The word 'selling' can bring up a lot of feelings, fears, and assumptions that we need to address.

I know that when I started my own business, the concept of selling and marketing my business did NOT come naturally.

I believed that I had to do what a lot of brick-and-mortar businesses do... TV ads, radio ads, paid advertising.

I also believed that I had to really push for people to buy. To sell, sell, sell!

I believed that it was my responsibility whether someone bought my offers or not.

But none of this is true. As a business owner, our only responsibility (when it comes to making money in our business) is presenting the opportunity for people to buy from us on a regular basis. That's it.

We're not here to convince people to buy from us.

It's not our responsibility whether someone buys our offers or not.

It's simply about ensuring that we are being specific enough in who the offers are for.

That we are providing enough information — we are presenting the opportunity enough times — for someone to decide: Yes or no.

Our only responsibility is to present the opportunity for someone to buy from us every day, and then ensure that we're providing enough information (value) for our ideal customers to make a decision.

What we don't want is people sitting on the fence.

So, present the opportunity often, drop the need to try and convince people to buy and people will buy.

As business owners, we're here to help. We're here to support. We're here to give our ideal customers as much information as they need to decide.

We're here to make it as easy as possible for someone to buy from us. That's all that we are responsible for doing.

Ok. I'm off my soapbox now.

I'm certain that the question that's now bubbling up for you is HOW... *How do I 'present the opportunity'?*

That's what we're going to cover next.

Presenting the opportunity

In this part of your SELLING activities, we're going to look at this from our Human Design strategy lens.

Our strategy is ultimately how we bring things to life.

So, before you start presenting the opportunity, check-in with yourself and ensure that you've created your offers following your strategy and authority first.

Be honest. The only person you're hurting is yourself if you aren't...

Because here's the thing: If you haven't done that—if you haven't created offers in this way, or you haven't followed the 'get paid to create' framework—then everything you do when it comes to selling your offers is gonna fall flat.

I'm not sugar coating this. It's too important.

This is the point in a game of Monopoly where you do NOT pass Go if you haven't followed your strategy and authority.

Circle back to the main book, *Cultivate You!* if you need a refresher.

Ok. Ready? Let's go.

MANIFESTORS: Your strategy is to INFORM. Unapologetically sharing what you feel the urge to create and move forward with.

In your SELLING activities, when presenting the opportunity for people to buy from you, this looks like ensuring that when you're informing, whether that's via email, social media, or whatever medium you're using to connect with your audience, you're providing a link to your offer(s) as well, at the end of your content.

The wording you might use could look like this:

"I'm bursting at the seams to get this into your hands. If you're onboard with what I've said, come and check out xxx".

GENERATORS: Your strategy is to RESPOND. To respond to external ideas, to the things that the Universe puts in front of you.

In your SELLING activities, when presenting the opportunity for people to buy from you, this looks like ensuring that you provide your audience with the opportunity to RESPOND to your ideas.

Provide your audience with options to choose from when you're sharing content with them *in response* to the offers you've created.
So, when you share a blog post, podcast episode, or YouTube video with them, or inside your emails... the wording you might use could look like this:

"If this resonated with you, here are [x number] ways I can support you right now:

1. *Xxx offer*
2. *Abc offer.*
3. *123 offers"*

MANIFESTING GENERATORS: Your strategy is to RESPOND and INFORM.

In your SELLING activities, when presenting the opportunity for people to buy from you, this looks like ensuring that when you're informing (after *responding*), whether that's via email, social media, or whatever medium you're using to connect with your audience, you're providing a link to your offer(s).

The wording you might use could look like this:

"If this resonated with you and if you're excited by what I've said, here's how you can dive deeper xxx".

PROJECTORS: Your strategy is to be INVITED. This means that before you give advice, you've got to wait for the person to ask for it.

In your SELLING activities, your approach is a little different. You're not designed to chase sales. Instead, you're designed to share your knowledge, insights, and wisdom.

Every time you do this, you create an opportunity for your audience to INVITE you to share your offers with them.

For you, every piece of content that you put out into the world needs to be optimized to bring people to your offer(s) or to join a waitlist (you'd use a waitlist for any new offers).

The wording you might use could look like this:

"If you feel seen, heard, and recognized by what I just shared, then I invite you to [join/check out/learn more about] xxx".

REFLECTORS: Your strategy is to FOLLOW THE LUNAR CYCLE. Because you're so open, you're being more carried along by the Universe rather than being directed like the other types.

In your SELLING activities, when it comes to presenting the opportunity, you'll want to optimize your content to link to your offer(s) or invite people to join your email list (or community, depending on your profile numbers).

The wording you might use could look like this:

"If you experienced the sensation of "wow, it's like xxx is in my head, how does she KNOW this?" then you will benefit from xxx".

I also encourage all of you to include in your emails, especially your newsletters, what I like to call the "soft sell P.S.".

You can craft this however you wish, but it might look like this:

P.S.: When you're ready, here's three ways I can support you right now:

- *If your next step is to build your email list, come join the List Building Collective [hyperlink]*
- *If you need daily feedback loops, peer support, and bi-monthly coaching, the Cultivate Group Program [hyperlink] is your best next step.*
- *If you're more of a DIY kinda gal, then subscribing to my YouTube channel [hyperlink] where you can binge watch everything is your best option*

There are many ways you can write this... You can even present it as an image (like this one I used to use):

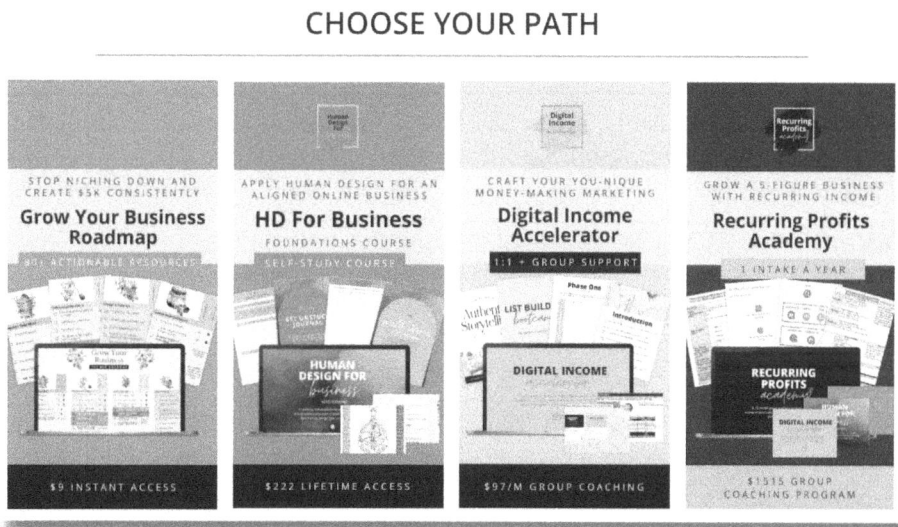

Bottom line: present the opportunity every day for people to buy from you and people WILL buy from YOU... when they are ready.

But what if you want to amplify this process? What if you want to automate your sales so that they are coming in on a regular, consistent basis?

Let's look at the next SELLING activity.

Automation and paid ads

To be clear, at a minimum, implementing the 'present the opportunity' into your business is something that makes sense for everyone. It's easy and fun!

But I know that a lot of you will be like me... looking to create more certainty around their income.

So, let's look at what that could be.

If we look at this through the lens of Human Design, most of us are not designed to chase sales.

So, setting up some type of automated way to make sales makes sense.

In terms of paid ads, this is where retargeting becomes your best friend... but I'm getting ahead of myself!

Let's start with the automation piece.

There are several ways to approach this.

You can set up funnels.

You can set up automated email sequences.

You can set up triggers to perform actions based on how someone interacts with your website...

But I like to keep things simple.

For me, I've focused on growing my email list. I'm not a huge fan of being on social media (it's just not my jive energetically), but I love writing and doing videos and sharing those with my email list.

It gives me a sense of community in a space that I've carefully curated. And there's no noise...

For me and the way I like to operate my business, I have automated email sequences that are triggered based on how someone enters my email list. You could call this an email funnel.

No matter your type, setting up an automated email sequence makes sense.

Here's what that flow looks like:

New person subscribes --> this triggers an email that delivers their freebie --> this then triggers an email automation (aka email funnel/sequence).

Depending on how the subscriber joins determines the type of email automation they receive.

Right now, you're probably scratching your head trying to understand what the heck I'm talking about... so let's dig into this a little deeper.

First, here's a visual view of this (continued on the next page):

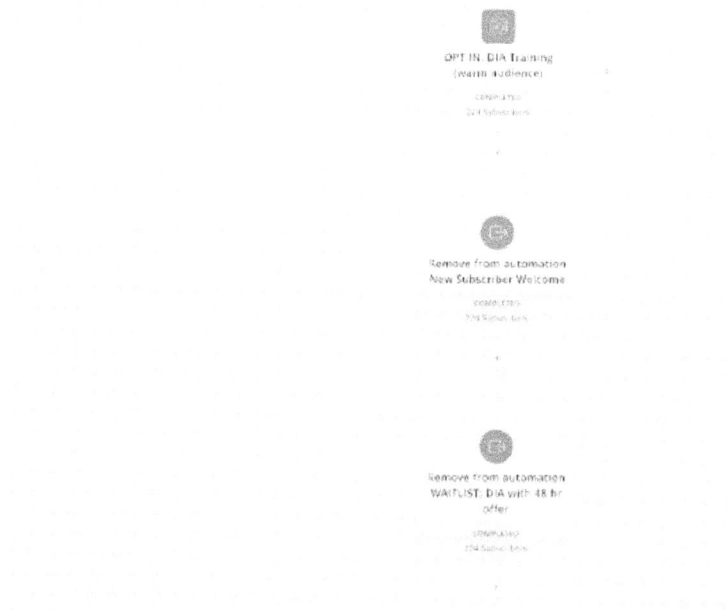

OPT IN: DIA Training
(warm Audience)

Remove from automation
New Subscriber Welcome

Remove from automation
WAITLIST: DIA with 48 hr
offer

Let's break this down further.

Step 1: Form (or you could trigger the automation with a tag being added or a sequence started)

In the example above, someone has joined my email list by opting in to grab a freebie. This means that they filled out a form with their name and email address to get that.

As part of this step, an automated email is triggered as soon as they sign up that delivers the freebie. This email is sent within 15 minutes of them signing up.

Step 2: Remove from New Subscriber Welcome automation

In my ConvertKit account, I have a welcome sequence automation set up that is triggered when any form is completed. If I'm wanting to delay or skip this process, I need to remove them from the automation. That's what this action step does.

Step 3: Sequence

This is the full automated sequence or email funnel that this subscriber is taken through. This particular sequence spans 33 days and has 14 emails that go out based on the timeframes set up.

While a subscriber is in this email funnel, they are NOT receiving my daily emails (newsletter).

This email funnel is part nurture / part sales, with the soft sell P.S. active in most emails.

Remember: it's about presenting the opportunity for people to buy from you regularly…

The goal of this sequence is to nurture my new person while also presenting the opportunity for them to join the Cultivate Group Coaching Program membership.

Two things can happen during the course of this email funnel:

1. If they purchase the membership while they are still in the email sequence, they will be pulled out of this sequence and added to the new member sequence for the Cultivate Group Coaching Program. They will also begin receiving my daily emails after 7 days of being a new member.
2. If they do not purchase the membership, they will then be tagged with STATUS: H&G Newsletter Sub and will begin receiving my daily emails.

RESOURCE: Simple Upsell Email Sequence *(available inside the Resource Hub here: https://www.hustleandgroove.com/cycresources).*

Whether someone buys or not is beside the point. The point of this email funnel is to familiarize my new subscribers with the way I run my business, what I believe, and how I can best help them.

They gain access to additional free resources and are guided through setting their business up to be easy, fun, and profitable.

This is one way I automate my sales for the *Cultivate Group Coaching Program*. My conversion rate is around 18% (at the time of printing this book).

The next part of my daily SELLING activities is retargeting.

My retargeting takes place on Facebook and Instagram as well as YouTube.

The beauty of retargeting is that you are simply putting your content in front of an audience who is already aware of you. These are often referred to as your WARM audience.

So, your budget is less, and you can speak using more direct language, more conversational.

My retargeting audiences look like this:

- I upload my email list (to Facebook) every 6 months.
- Facebook Page engagers last 365 days.
- Instagram Profile engagers last 365 days.
- Facebook/Instagram Lead Generation Form Engagers last 90 days.
- Website Visitors last 180 days.
- Video Views 25% last 180 days.

These are created as 'custom audiences'.

When I run a retargeting campaign, I stack all these audiences into one ad set.

I run retargeting ads at $1-$2 a day.

These ads could be to drive traffic to a new blog post, or video on my Facebook Page.

Sometimes they are conversion ads to my $9 "Grow Your Business $5k Roadmap".

The type of campaign you choose to run is up to you. There is no 'retargeting' campaign or ad type.

Retargeting simply refers to the audience you choose at the ad set level.

I have a video that walks through this in more detail that you can view here (accessible inside the resources hub).

When it comes to your daily SELLING activities, the number one thing to remember is that your job is simply to present the opportunity for people to buy from you.

It's not your job to convince them to buy.

It's not your responsibility to make sure they buy.

It's not your responsibility to make sure they buy.
All you are here to do is ensure that you provide enough information for your ideal customer to decide — yes or no.

Choose your SELLING activities based on your focus and energy and add them to your 90-Day Plan.

Optional: Setting up funnels

I debated with myself about whether to include a section on funnels... because at the end of the day, it's not so much about needing a funnel in place.

It's about ensuring you have an *ecosystem* that meets people where they are at.

That ecosystem looks like this:

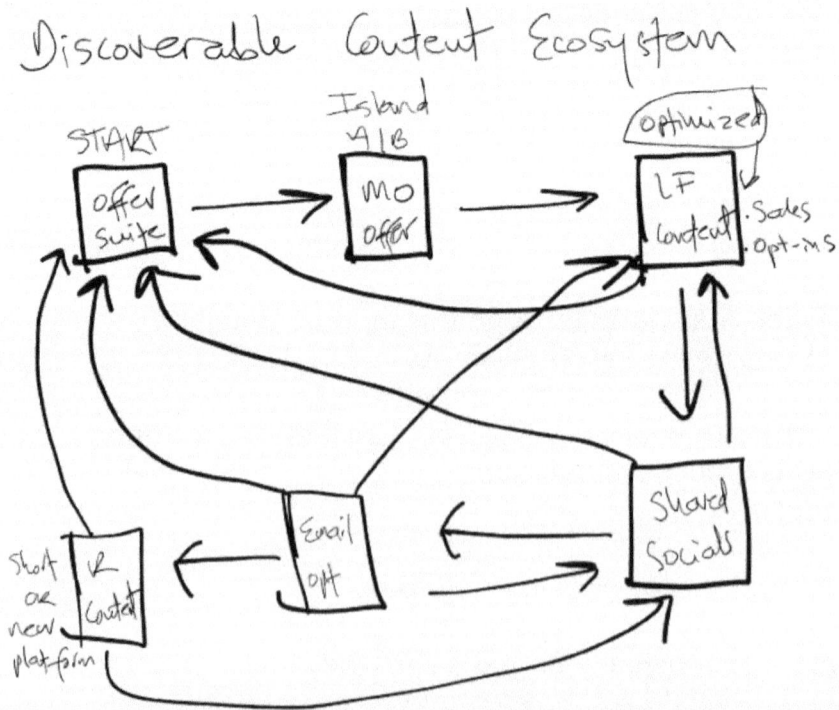

A funnel makes up such a small part of this.

As with the rest of the way I do things, I like to keep things simple.

I do not like funnels that constantly present offers after you've made an initial purchase... it's too much all in one go.

Instead, the approach I take is to think about things from my ideal customer's viewpoint...

If they are buying offer #1, do I have any additional offers that would help them implement offer #1 faster, or help them transition to the next step quicker?

Let's look at an example:

I have a $9 offer called the *Grow Your Business $5k Roadmap*.

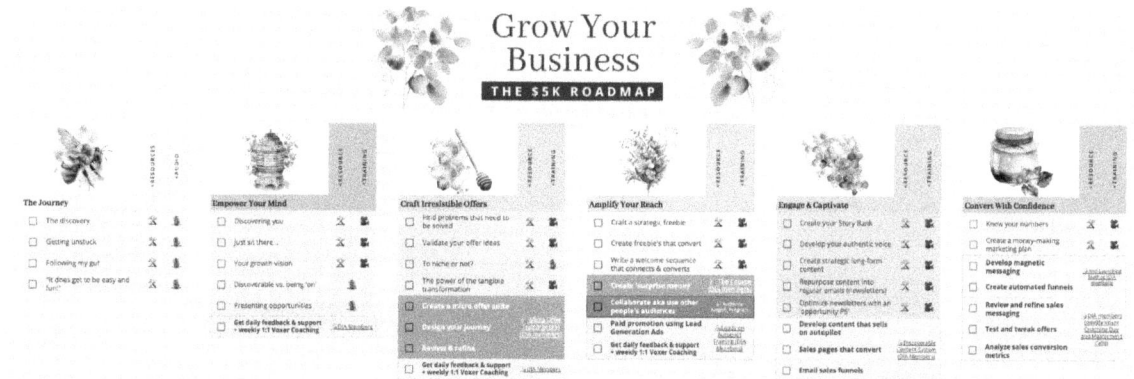

When someone reaches the checkout page for this offer, they will also see what is called an "order bump".

This is simply an additional offer that they can purchase at the same time.

It's two offers on one checkout page (as shown in the example on the next page).

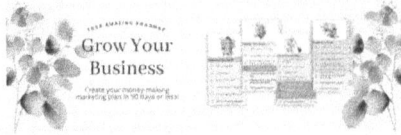

Grow Your Business

Create your money making marketing plan in 90 days or less!

Here's what you're getting:

- ✓ 40+ audio and video trainings
- ✓ 40+ templates, tools, resources, copy, examples and more
- ✓ Step-by-step action plan
- ✓ Progress tracker
- ✓ Lifetime access to the trainings, tools, and resources included inside the roadmap

---

Get instant access now for just $9 USD!

CONTACT INFORMATION

| lisecarter@gmail.com |
| lisecarter@gmail.com |

| First Name | Last Name |

BILLING ADDRESS

| Street Address | City |
| State/Region | Zip/Post Code |

Australia

PAYMENT INFORMATION

VISA - xxxx - xxxx - xxxx - 4005

☐ **Yes, add the Get Paid to Create training too!**

LIMITED TIME ONLY: Access the **Get Paid to Create** training for just **$27** (normally $47). Join 250+ students and learn the step-by-step framework that allows you to pre-sell your offers BEFORE you create them. Never launch an offer again to crickets. Get paid to create instead! This training pairs perfectly with The $5k Roadmap, allowing you to get up and running faster.

G Pay

ORDER SUMMARY

| Grow Your Business Roadmap | $9.00 |
| Total | $9.00 |

Yes! I'm Ready to Get Started Now

SSL CHECKOUT

The order bump offer is my mini course *Get Paid to Create*. It's priced at $27 on this checkout page (it's normally $47 or free if you're a T.C.M. member).

Once my ideal customer purchases the roadmap and/or both offers together, they are taken to another sales page where they are invited to join the *List Building Collective* membership.

This sales page has a video for them to watch that explains what the List Building Collective is and who it's for.

This is a one-click upsell sales page. This simply means that if they choose to join the *List Building Collective* at this time, they will *not* have to enter their credit card details in again.

If they click on the purchase button, it will add the membership to their existing order.

If they decide that the *List Building Collective* isn't right for them right now, they have the option to click a link that says, *"No thanks. Take me to the roadmap."*

The next page they see is the page to access the roadmap.

They will also receive an email with access details there, too, no matter what they purchase.

You do NOT need to have anything like this in place.

But where possible, I do recommend having an order bump on your checkout page.

Especially if you genuinely have offers that complement each other or provide the next step for your customer.

There is no right or wrong way to approach this. Follow your strategy and authority.

Or simply... do what *feels* easy and fun for you.

My hope for you, dear reader, is that you now feel inspired and hopeful.

Inspired to run your business in a way that feels good to you. That leverages your you-nique gifts, strengths, and talents.

Hopeful that you can have a business that's profitable when you simply follow the things that are easy and fun for you and ditch the things that are not.

Everything and anything works in a business when the person running it is aligned.

You got this!

SELLING Daily Activities

exercise time

Now that you've got your GROW and NURTURE activities dialed in, it's time to talk about what your daily SELLING activities might be.

<table>
<tr><td>YOUR RESPONSIBILITY</td><td>Our only responsibility is to present the opportunity for someone to buy from us every day, and then ensure that we're providing enough information (value) for our ideal customers to make a decision.</td></tr>
</table>

Presenting the opportunity for people to buy from you every day looks like optimizing your emails, your blog content, video content, Podcast, etc.

Jot down how you'll "present the opportunity" for people to buy from you daily aka what will you do to set up the opportunity for sales in your business each day?

Refer back to your strategy and authority for ideas:

SELLING Daily Activities

exercise time

Along with presenting the opportunity daily, you can also run paid ads, set up funnels etc. If you need ideas checkout the main book, *Cultivate You!* for a full breakdown, including based on your type. Jot down your intentions below and don't forget to incorporate them into your 90-Day Plan.

CHAPTER FOUR

your 90-day money-making plan

ideas...

ideas...

You might be wondering… why 90 days? Why not 12 months?

My hope is that by now, you understand much more about how you're designed to interact with the world.

Through that lens, you'll see that none of us are really designed to have things set in stone.

The only type that might benefit from having a marketing plan beyond 90 days is a Generator who has one specific zone of genius.

For the rest of us, we need flexibility. We need the space to follow our energy.

Of course, it's your business. You get to decide what this looks like.

My recommendation is that you simply plan the next 90 days and then if you feel called to do so, map out the next.

There is no right or wrong way to do this. Only what *feels* **easy** and **fun** for you!

Part of setting up your you-nique marketing system is understanding the types of activities that best work with your energy type in Human Design.

Combined with your profile numbers, your type, strategy, and authority can help you determine what might work for you when it comes to marketing strategies.

So let's dig a little deeper and consider what our marketing activities *could* look like.

No matter your type, strategy, or authority, you'll want to choose your top 3-5 favorite ways to show up for your audience.

Depending on what feels aligned, I recommend focusing on one social media platform plus your email list.

Reminder: You don't need to be on social media all the time to use it in your business.

Remember, marketing is simply communication with a clear call to action.

MANIFESTORS: Schedule your informing content across social platforms while only showing up on one intentionally (if you feel called to do so).

This might look something like this:

- Do a post/live in your Facebook Group/private community 1 x / week (or less frequently, it's up to you).

- Write a long-form email 1 / month (or record a video or audio if you don't want to write it and use software to transcribe it into an email).

Repurpose the Facebook post/live and long-form email into:

- 1-4 Emails / month (you decide how often you're emailing your list).

- 20 Instagram posts / month (or whatever other social media platform(s) you want to share. This is not you showing up; this is simply sharing content) — OUTSOURCE the image creation and schedule the posts in advance! Or use AI tools to help you repurpose faster.

- 1 Facebook group post / week.

This is your consistent, ongoing marketing activities in between any intentional launches or monthly promotions you might have.

Any evergreen funnels you've got going might include some of this content too.

GENERATORS: Schedule your content to be shared across social platforms while only showing up on one intentionally.

You are your brand, so the more your audience sees and hears from you, the better.

This might look something like this:

- Do a post/live in your Facebook Group 2 x/ week.

- Write a blog post 2 x/ month.

- Record a YouTube video 1 x/ week (works best if you have a Defined Throat Center).

Repurpose this content into:

- 1-4 Emails / month (you decide how often you're emailing your list).

- 20 social media posts / month — OUTSOURCE the image creation and schedule the posts in advance! OR use AI tools to help you repurpose faster.

- 1 mini-training for your clients / month (could be audio or video or workbook).

This is your consistent, ongoing marketing activities in between any intentional launches or monthly promotions you might have.

Any evergreen funnels you've got going might include some of this content, too.

MANIFESTING GENERATORS: Schedule your content to be shared across social platforms while only showing up on one (or two) intentionally.

You are your brand, so the more your audience sees and hears from you, the better.

This might look something like this:

- Do a live in your Facebook Group 5 x/ week.

- Write 1-2 posts/ month for your FB page / Instagram / LinkedIn profiles.

- Record a YouTube video 1 x/ week.

- Host a weekly Voxer Q&A session.

- Offer a Zoom call once a month.

Repurpose this content into:

- 1-4 Emails / month (you decide how often you're emailing your list).

- 20 social media posts / month — OUTSOURCE the image creation and schedule the posts in advance! Use AI tools to repurpose faster.

- 1-2 masterclasses / workshops for your clients / month.

- Workbook to sell from your website and/or Amazon.

- Templates and swipe files for your offers.

This is your consistent, ongoing marketing activities in between any intentional launches or monthly promotions you might have.

Any evergreen funnels you've got going might include some of this content too.

PROJECTORS: As a Projector, you're simply sharing your zone of genius so that people can invite you (aka buy your stuff!). Schedule-block the creation process into your 90-day plan weekly or monthly.

Use a tool like Buffer.com to schedule your content to be shared across social platforms while only showing up on one intentionally as you feel drawn to do so.

This might look something like this:

- Video every week on YouTube (works best if you have a Defined Throat Center).

- Write a blog post 1 x / week.

Repurpose the blog post/video into:

- 1-4 Emails / month (you decide how often you're emailing your list).

- 25 social media posts / month — OUTSOURCE the image creation and schedule the posts in advance! Use AI tools to repurpose even faster and to help you develop content. You need to be SEEN for the invitation to take place, don't—forget that.

This is your consistent, ongoing marketing activities in between any intentional launches you might have.

Any evergreen funnels you've got going might include some of this content too.

REFLECTORS: Schedule-block the creation process into your 90-day plan weekly or monthly and create on the days you feel energized to do so.

Use a tool like Buffer.com to schedule your content to be shared across social platforms while only showing up on one intentionally as you feel excited to do so.

This might look something like this (you'd likely batch this content instead of doing it in the moment):

- Write a blog post 1-4 x / month.

- Write an email 1 x / month.

- Record an audio for your private community (based on your profile numbers — I'm speaking to all the 4s here!)

Repurpose the blog posts and long-form email into:

- 25+ social media posts / month — OUTSOURCE the image creation and schedule the posts in advance! Use AI tools to do this faster.

- Some type of live video or audio when you're energetically aligned (this will depend on your Throat center gates being activated by the transits).

This is your consistent, ongoing marketing activities in between any intentional launches you might have.

Any evergreen funnels you've got going might include some of this content too.

Now that you've got some ideas about what your marketing activities might look like, let's create your 90-day money-making marketing plan.

Before you do that, you'll need to answer the following questions:

How am I feeling right now, at this moment? Aligned, excited about my business? Or am I anxious and worried, not sure what's going on?

Over the next 30 days, what would I love to be doing in my business? What offer excites me the most?

Do I have any commitments that I need to schedule into my 90-day plan? This might include collaboration giveaways, summits, bundles, or affiliate promotions. Am I going to be away from my business at all?

The next questions are based on each type:

As a **Manifestor**, where are my energy levels at? Do I have my 200% surge to move something forward? Or am I in the 50% - 20% phase where I need to rest? This will be the overarching influence for at least the next 30 days, so pay attention to what you're committing to.

As a **Generator**, where are my energy levels at? Am I feeling excited about my plans? Do I feel like I could work in my business 24/7? This will be the overarching influence for at least the next 30-90 days, so pay attention to what you're committing to.

As a **Manifesting Generator**, where are my energy levels at? What's lighting me up and propelling me forward right now? This will be the overarching influence for at least the next 30 days, so pay attention to what you're committing to.

As a **Projector**, where are my energy levels at? What am I excited about to move forward with? How much time do I need to get stuff into place? This will be the overarching influence for at least the next 30 days, so pay attention to what you're committing to.

As a **Reflector**, where are my energy levels at? What transits are impacting my chart right now? What can I expect things to look like over the next 30 days and how can I plan to move things forward based on my energy ebb and flows? This will be the overarching influence for at least the next 30 days, so pay attention to what you're committing to.

Once you've answered those questions, this final question is the decision-maker...

Following my strategy and authority, what do I feel called to do?

90-day plans are designed to be flexible in nature. You don't have to have every day mapped out.

The intention is to start with a working plan and then tweak and adjust based on your own way of doing business.

For example, my 90-day plan starts out fairly mapped out:

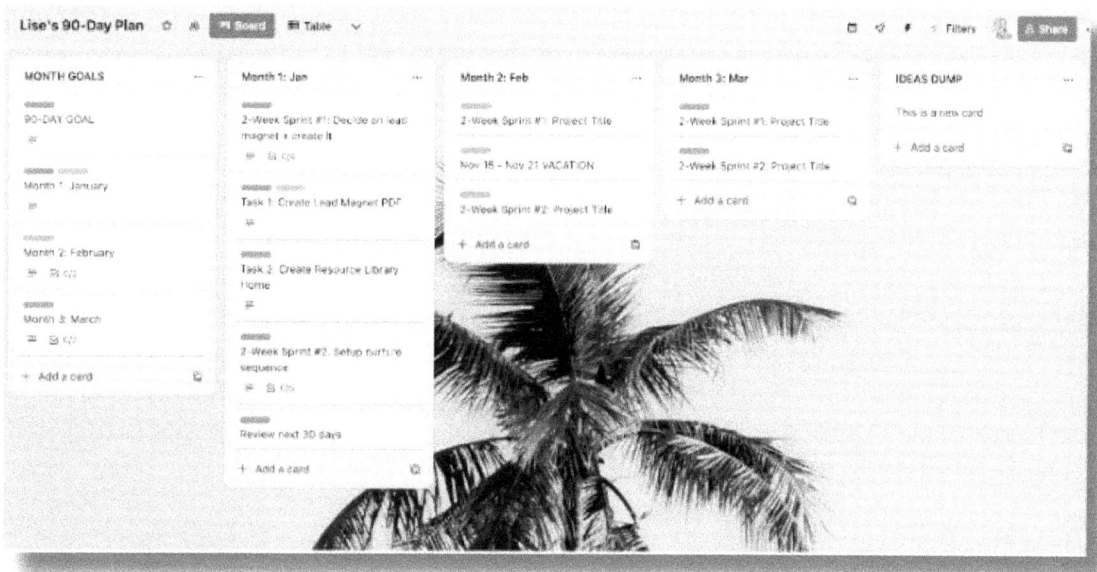

But as each two-week sprint goes on, I'll adjust and make tweaks as needed.

There are two ways to create your 90-day plan:

1. Pick a goal for each month (or one goal mapped out over the 90 days) to focus on and create daily or weekly action steps; OR
2. Pick a goal for each month (or one goal mapped out over the 90 days) to focus on and create 2-week sprints (like mini projects) that have a specific focus.

RESOURCES: Trello 90-Day Plan template and walk-through video + 90-Day Growth Planner PDF - 30 Days *(available inside the Resource Hub here: https://www.hustleandgroove.com/cycresources)*.

The key is to review your plans weekly to make changes and adjustments as needed.

You can also simply write down your goals and daily action steps in a planner. As I said, there is no right or wrong way to do this.

You don't even need to have a 90-day plan. It could be a 30-day plan.

The whole point of this exercise is to have your eyes on your business. If you don't have clear intentions for marketing your business, then how are you going to make money?

Remember how I said that for the first eight or so years in my business, I was in a feast or famine cycle?

The main reason for that was that I didn't have any intentions in place to market my business.

I didn't look at my numbers. I had no idea how I was making money.

You always get to decide how you run your business. At a minimum, know your numbers...

RESOURCE: Income Projection Calculator (available inside the resource hub).

Now that we've got our you-nique marketing plan in place, let's dive into this deeper and look at what your daily money-making activities look like.

This is where you get to follow your strategy and authority the most.

As you exit this section, take a minute to regroup and ask yourself this question:

How am I feeling about my business right now?

Create your 90-Day Plan following your strategy and authority (what you're committing to for the next 90 days) and then incorporate your daily money-making activities as well.

90-Day Plan
exercise time

GOAL/FOCUS AREA	30 DAYS	60 DAYS	90 DAYS
Write down your main goals or focus for the next 90 days here.	For each 30 day timeframe, list all the tasks that need to happen to help you achieve your goals within the next 90 days.		
Write and publish my next book!	• Mindmap + Outline book • Decide on structure • Set writing targets	• Self-edit • Get edited • Cover design • Formatted for ebook and print	• Build launch team • Decide on promotions • Proof copy of book • Hit publish!

90-Day Plan

exercise time

GOAL/FOCUS AREA	30 DAYS	60 DAYS	90 DAYS
Write down your main goals or focus for the next 90 days here.	For each 30 day timeframe, list all the tasks that need to happen to help you achieve your goals within the next 90 days.		
Write and publish my next book!	• Mindmap + Outline book • Decide on structure • Set writing targets	• Self-edit • Get edited • Cover design • Formatted for ebook and print	• Build launch team • Decide on promotions • Proof copy of book • Hit publish!

90-Day Plan
exercise time

Need more space? Jot down your intentions below and know that you can change direction at any time!

NOW WHAT?

your next steps...

You Made It!

what to do next...

By now, this workbook + planning guide should be full to the brim with your ideas, creative thoughts, answers to your burning questions and as many scribbles as needed to get you to this point.

My intention with this workbook was to provide you with the space to explore more concepts not covered inside the companion book, **Cultivate You!:** *Harness Your Strengths, Craft Your Message, and Market With Ease!*

It does get to be easy and fun… AND profitable!

Once you've completed all the exercises, all that's left is to take action, create your 90-day plan and then get to it.

To kickstart you off you'll find pages following this section to help you map out your first 30 days. Use this space to jot down ideas or plan out your intentions for incorporating your Human Design chart into your business.

Don't forget to access extra templates and resources via the **Resource Hub**, which you'll find here: https://www.hustleandgroove.com/cycresources.

You might also be starting to feel *#allthefeels*… and a few new fears, challenges, and limiting beliefs are rearing their ugly heads.

It's likely that these fears, challenges, and limiting beliefs are centered around the selling of your offers. You're probably judging yourself, thinking: *"Who will buy what I've created?"*

Or you might be experiencing decision fatigue, overwhelm, and plain ole *"I don't know what to do!"* syndrome.

If that's you, then you might like to check out the entire *Cultivate Your Business Book Series.* You'll find these all on Amazon here: https://geni.us/cybbseries.

You Made It!

what to do next...

What's your marketing persona?!

If you want to dive into your own you-nique marketing persona, take the **Marketing Persona Quiz!**

You'll find that here: https://hustleandgroove.com/mpquiz

And if you didn't get a chance to check out the main book, *Cultivate You!*, you can grab that on Amazon in both Kindle or Paperback here: https://www.hustleandgroove.com/cybbook

Good luck with it all and thanks so much for sharing your knowledge and expertise with the world.

We need people like you sharing what they know.

I'd also love it if you took this time to leave a review on Amazon. You can let me know what you liked and what you didn't like right there.

Or alternatively, shoot me an email with your feedback: lise@hustleandgroove.com.

And remember, you got this!

About The Author

meet Lise Cartwright

Lise Cartwright is a bestselling author and creative business coach who is obsessed with helping others create and grow a business and life they love!

She loves curling up on a comfy couch with a good book, a hot cup of Chai Latte, and the soothing sounds of waves crashing against the white sandy beaches of the Gold Coast, Australia.

She's the founder of **www.hustleandgroove.com**, the #1 online resource for getting clear on your business model and growing an online business you are excited to work in. Her business motto is: *"if it's not easy and fun, why do it?!"*

Through her books, training videos, and coaching, she's helped thousands of people on their journey to creating an online business that's **easy**, **fun**, and **profitable**.

You can connect with Lise on the following social media platforms:

f FACEBOOK.COM/HUSTLEANDGROOVE   **in** LINKEDIN.COM/IN/LISECARTWRIGHT

◎ INSTAGRAM.COM/LISECARTWRIGHTNZ

If your actions create a legacy that inspires others to dream more, learn more, do more, and become more, you're an excellent leader.

DOLLY PARTON

YOUR 30 DAY
plan for success

My Next 30 Days

what's your focus?

FOCUS:

My strategy is to: _____

My immediate next steps are:

_____

_____

_____

_____

_____

_____

_____

_____

_____

_____

_____

_____

_____

_____

My Next 30 Days

what's your focus?

FOCUS:

My strategy is to: _____

My immediate next steps are:

_____

_____

_____

_____

_____

_____

_____

_____

_____

_____

_____

_____

_____

My Next 30 Days

what's your focus?

FOCUS:

My strategy is to: _____

My immediate next steps are:

_____

_____

_____

_____

_____

_____

_____

_____

_____

_____

_____

_____

_____

_____

_____

My Next 30 Days

what's your focus?

FOCUS:

My strategy is to: _____

My immediate next steps are:

_____

_____

_____

_____

_____

_____

_____

_____

_____

_____

_____

_____

_____

_____

My Next 30 Days

what's your focus?

FOCUS:

My strategy is to: _____

My immediate next steps are:

_____

_____

_____

_____

_____

_____

_____

_____

_____

_____

_____

_____

_____

_____

_____

My Next 30 Days

what's your focus?

FOCUS:

My strategy is to: _____

My immediate next steps are:

_____

_____

_____

_____

_____

_____

_____

_____

_____

_____

_____

_____

_____

_____

My Next 30 Days

what's your focus?

FOCUS:

My strategy is to: _____

My immediate next steps are:

_____

_____

_____

_____

_____

_____

_____

_____

_____

_____

_____

_____

_____

_____

_____

_____

My Next 30 Days

what's your focus?

FOCUS:

My strategy is to: _____

My immediate next steps are:

_____

_____

_____

_____

_____

_____

_____

_____

_____

_____

_____

_____

_____

_____

My Next 30 Days

what's your focus?

FOCUS:

My strategy is to: _____

My immediate next steps are:

_____

_____

_____

_____

_____

_____

_____

_____

_____

_____

_____

_____

_____

_____

_____

My Next 30 Days

what's your focus?

FOCUS:

My strategy is to: _____

My immediate next steps are:

_____

_____

_____

_____

_____

_____

_____

_____

_____

_____

_____

_____

_____

_____

My Next 30 Days

what's your focus?

FOCUS:

My strategy is to: _____

My immediate next steps are:

_____
_____
_____
_____
_____
_____
_____
_____
_____
_____
_____
_____
_____
_____
_____
_____
_____

My Next 30 Days

what's your focus?

FOCUS:

My strategy is to: _____

My immediate next steps are:

_____

_____

_____

_____

_____

_____

_____

_____

_____

_____

_____

_____

_____

_____

My Next 30 Days

what's your focus?

FOCUS:

My strategy is to: _____

My immediate next steps are:

_____

_____

_____

_____

_____

_____

_____

_____

_____

_____

_____

_____

_____

_____

My Next 30 Days

what's your focus?

FOCUS:

My strategy is to: _____

My immediate next steps are:

_____

_____

_____

_____

_____

_____

_____

_____

_____

_____

_____

_____

_____

My Next 30 Days

what's your focus?

FOCUS:

My strategy is to: _____

My immediate next steps are:

_____

_____

_____

_____

_____

_____

_____

_____

_____

_____

_____

_____

_____

_____

_____

My Next 30 Days

what's your focus?

FOCUS:

My strategy is to: _____

My immediate next steps are:

_____

_____

_____

_____

_____

_____

_____

_____

_____

_____

_____

_____

_____

_____

_____

My Next 30 Days

what's your focus?

FOCUS:

My strategy is to: _____

My immediate next steps are:

_____

_____

_____

_____

_____

_____

_____

_____

_____

_____

_____

_____

_____

_____

_____

_____

_____

My Next 30 Days

what's your focus?

FOCUS:

My strategy is to: _____

My immediate next steps are:

_____

_____

_____

_____

_____

_____

_____

_____

_____

_____

_____

_____

_____

My Next 30 Days

what's your focus?

FOCUS:

My strategy is to: _____

My immediate next steps are:

_____

_____

_____

_____

_____

_____

_____

_____

_____

_____

_____

_____

_____

_____

_____

_____

My Next 30 Days

what's your focus?

FOCUS:

My strategy is to: _____

My immediate next steps are:

_____

_____

_____

_____

_____

_____

_____

_____

_____

_____

_____

_____

_____

My Next 30 Days

what's your focus?

FOCUS:

My strategy is to: _____

My immediate next steps are:

_____

_____

_____

_____

_____

_____

_____

_____

_____

_____

_____

_____

_____

_____

_____

_____

My Next 30 Days

what's your focus?

FOCUS:

My strategy is to: _____

My immediate next steps are:

_____

_____

_____

_____

_____

_____

_____

_____

_____

_____

_____

_____

_____

_____

My Next 30 Days

what's your focus?

FOCUS:

My strategy is to: _____

My immediate next steps are:

_____

_____

_____

_____

_____

_____

_____

_____

_____

_____

_____

_____

_____

_____

My Next 30 Days
what's your focus?

FOCUS:

My strategy is to: _____

My immediate next steps are:

_____

_____

_____

_____

_____

_____

_____

_____

_____

_____

_____

_____

_____

_____

My Next 30 Days

what's your focus?

FOCUS:

My strategy is to: _____

My immediate next steps are:

_____

_____

_____

_____

_____

_____

_____

_____

_____

_____

_____

_____

_____

_____

_____

_____

My Next 30 Days

what's your focus?

FOCUS:

My strategy is to: _____

My immediate next steps are:

_____

_____

_____

_____

_____

_____

_____

_____

_____

_____

_____

_____

_____

_____

My Next 30 Days

what's your focus?

FOCUS:

My strategy is to: _____

My immediate next steps are:

_____
_____
_____
_____
_____
_____
_____
_____
_____
_____
_____
_____
_____
_____
_____
_____
_____

My Next 30 Days

what's your focus?

FOCUS:

My strategy is to: _____

My immediate next steps are:

_____

_____

_____

_____

_____

_____

_____

_____

_____

_____

_____

_____

_____

_____

My Next 30 Days

what's your focus?

FOCUS:

My strategy is to: _____

My immediate next steps are:

_____

_____

_____

_____

_____

_____

_____

_____

_____

_____

_____

_____

_____

_____

_____

_____

_____

My Next 30 Days

what's your focus?

FOCUS:

My strategy is to: _____

My immediate next steps are:

_____

_____

_____

_____

_____

_____

_____

_____

_____

_____

_____

_____

_____

Nothing has meaning except for the meaning I give it...

JIM FONTIN

Notes
capture your ideas

Notes

capture your ideas